Kaleidoscope

Also by Margo Poirier and published by Ginninderra Press
Unzipped
A Previous Life

Margo Poirier

Kaleidoscope
The way I see it

Kaleidoscope: The way I see it
ISBN 978 1 76109 266 4
Copyright © Margo Poirier 2022

First published 2022 by
Ginninderra Press
PO Box 3461 Port Adelaide 5015
www.ginninderrapress.com.au

Contents

Cock of the Walk	7
Musings	8
Rooted	9
Sod It	11
Stone the Crows, Is That It?	12
When I Am Old	14
The Enabler	15
The End	16
Silly Poems	17
Protest	21
Propinquity	22
The Star Strangled Banner	23
No Use	24
More Silly Poetry	25
Look Up	26
In Days of Old	27
Flight Path	29
Fairy Tales Retold	30
Eye Blot After Drops	34
Dusty the Undaunted: an Australian Ballad	35
Wild	37
Vicious	38
Wombat Black	40
Rivers of Tears and Fears	41
Natural Anthem	42
Argelès-sur-Mer	43
The Spider Saw It All	45

Cock of the Walk

He comes from a land asunder
Where the Covid rules in big blunder!
Beneath veranda hair and fake tan
Lies the quintessential Stars and Stripy fake man.

He's immune to truth and common sensing,
Has an interest in walls and wire fencing.
Who will save us from this bondage?
Might just as well eat a Vegemite sandwich!

So you'd better run, you'd better take cover.
Cockwomble sure ain't our blood brother.

Musings

The muse has gone
she left today
she warned that she would go away

I'm now bereft
of thought and word
which I know must surely seem absurd.

But there it is
in white and black –
and I wonder if she's coming back.

Rooted

He
was like the
super moon
full-bodied,
brilliantly
abnormally
yellow and
beyond belief.

Doubting Tomasina
me, but
there he was,
glowing
in my face,
happier than
anyone had a right
to be.

The skin
on my face
tightened,
squeaking in its
taut shimmer.

I
was
moonstruck,
struck dumb
as I stood
without a shadow
and
without a
shadow of a doubt,
unable to move,
rooted
to the proverbial
spot.

Sod It

Here I lie beneath the sod
somewhere between the devil and god.
In honesty, the room is sparse
with little light and short of grass.

I mustn't complain, too late for that
I had my runs while in to bat,
and now I'm well out of the eleven
it's up the stairs and into heaven.

Stone the Crows, Is That It?

It's true, you know that dead is dead
I didn't believe it until I read
that life eventually ceases to be
for everyone, including me!

I have led a truly blessed life
I did not beat nor harass my wife,
I worked with honesty and toil
was hardly ever off the boil.

How come, then, I have bought the farm,
I think as I lie with some alarm
and peer at these four walls of dirt
around which I am stiffly girt.

It happened, quick, in proverbial blink,
somewhere between the fridge and sink,
I dropped real quick onto the floor
then straight on through that deathly door.

A big surprise is always fun
but not like this particular one!
Stone the crows, a bloke needs a nod
before he stands in the queue to God.

But truthfully, I have to say,
he's not a bad bloke, in his different way.
He looks real kind, has lots of hair
but he wears a dress, I do declare

he's not at all what I thought I'd see
between the gatepost, you and me.
I think he's a bit behind the times
and hark at all those bloody chimes!

But as I sit on my personal cloud
I can't help feeling personally proud.
That I John Doe have a personal front seat
And, personally, I think that's pretty neat!

AMEN

When I Am Old

When I am old(er)
I will walk, still,
but with a smart, sturdy stick.
I, a humble sophisticate, will
hold this accoutrement, this
thrusting, wielding, poking, point making,
multi-purpose artefact proudly…
my walking companion, person filter,
incognito prop and bird offensive.
My paper stabber, activist jabber,
at the ready.
Physical support?
Oh, don't be silly!

The Enabler

Yes, I am the enabler,
I do not do the deed
but always I'm available
whenever there's a need.

I hide between the shadows
waiting for the chance
to sit astride with misplaced pride
the poisoned, guilty lance.

The End

How quickly she becomes
'The Body' the minute
life is extinguished.
Quicker than a slippery turd,
anonymous as a shadow.
Deceased, passed, moved on,
shuffled off the mortal coil,
off the boil
like an old kettle
gone, left us,
Died…
perhaps less ambiguous!
Or she's gone.

She died peacefully in her sleep
aided by a cocktail of life ending drugs!
At peace now…dead = not living = peace,
not dormant until next spring, but
part of winter's mulch and here's the rub –
the blossom in September could be the returning
of the body, at least in part and in
glorious technicolour.

The Beginning

Silly Poems

1

Writing poetry can give me the shits
especially when words come in pieces and bits.
The muse sometimes comes on a prayer or a whim
but usually only when I am not in.

There's a slit in the curtain through which I can see
my jeans on the clothes line but not clothing me.
A branch newly dropped from the willow above
has ripped off the wings of a passing white dove.

The pink morning sky was blue then was white
which I know from experience will be different tonight.
A portion of rooftop is visible too
via the window I am now looking through.

So the pane in the frame
gives a preview of time
of a part of the day
that's exclusively mine.

2

The sun makes an entrance through the legs of my jeans
but my legs are not in them, they're still in between
and cocooned as I am within soft folds of doona
I cannot decide to rise later or sooner.

Day starts uncomfortably with insomniac cat
who claws at the window, eschewing her mat.
Catslaughter is tempting, her tormenting persistent.
If only my poetry could be so consistent!

3

There's milk from the cow
familiar and white,

milk from the goat
smelly and light.

Milk from the soya bean
greyish and thin,
milk from the camel
you'd cheerfully bin.

Milk from the yak
drunk by the brave,
milk from the buffalo
cheesy and grave.

But what about milk
from the ant or the slug
and how many milkings
would fill up a jug?

And while on the subject
of milk and of udders,
we're all being milked
by our government brudders!

4

The front door opes
as well it might
and doth give way
to ghostly fright

based purely on
some supposition
that someone calls
with proposition

Ah, no I find
on investigation
'tis cat perfecting
levitation.

Protest

Methinks we protest far too much,
it takes up too much time
when just the research can take weeks
between the casks of wine.

Now, here's a list from which to choose
and surely, choose you should
or you'll attract some looks of scorn
from those who 'work for good'.

Just disagree with everything
and everybody too,
Protest against the range of products
that you flush down the loo.

Protest that Labor's better
Protest that Liberals rock
Protest for vegan-labelled foods
and biodynamic socks!

Yes, there's a cause for all of us
so we should put our trust
in one more political party,
and a Minister for Dust.

Yep, dust is fucking everywhere
and I for one protest.
The banner just needs one more stitch
It's ban the dust or bust!

Propinquity

Forest of mint,
plantation of weeds,
they get along.

The Star Strangled Banner

Oh say can you see, as the light slowly wanes
from the famed oval office and its dulled windowpanes.
The broad stripes are thinning and the stars fade to grey,
all we see are reflections of a golden toupee.

The flag is now shivering as the mast starts to buckle
and the grip on the country is white at the knuckle.
The mutinous crew gnaw like rats in the beams,
the star strangled banner comes apart at the seams.

*

There is nothing to cushion the fall of the mighty,
nothing was saved for a bleak, rainy day.
Shares in umbrellas have soared through the rooftops,
the white house is empty; they've all gone away!

No Use

The milk keeps spilling
a never ending flood
spoiling everything.
I
could have stopped it
before the flood
if
I had stopped crying
when
it was just a trickle.

More Silly Poetry

Awake my brain to catch the train from platform number nine
I dreamed in sleep my thoughts to keep like onions steeped in brine.
Shakespeare wrote and here I quote about my solid flesh
Oh, it will thaw and long before the seasons start to mesh.

As onion skin when peeled reveals a virgin-glowing blue,
Thus do my thoughts discovered show a slightly different hue!
No virgin I, nor boundaries left, nor door or window closed,
The colours flood into my world as I have now composed

A poem so lacking in restraint, yet I was called to write,
I cannot stop the flow by day, nor stop the flow by night.
So here I am twixt dusk and dawn, in solitary mode
Needing one more bloody line before I hit the road!

Look Up

Treetops tickle the sky,
well trained fan dancers
allowing titillating glimpses
of virgin blue.

This magic, free to air
performance, plays
to global audiences.

Look up –
it's a whole new world.

In Days of Old

In days of old
when knights were bold
and armour made of tin,
then Ginger Meggs
with bandy legs
went out to fight for Min.

But that was then
now knights are few,
the playing field has altered.
We've stuck it out,
have dared to shout
with zeal that seldom faltered.

Our legs they may be bandy,
our voices tired and thin,
our faces wear the maps of life,
to show where we have been.

Wisdom warms our bellies now
and knowledge keeps us sharp,
sisterhood has arms of love
and patience when we carp.

We spend our love in buckets,
we laugh and keep it light.
The comforts we have battled for
sustain us in the night.

So do not judge an older soul
just look within the pages.
Read them when you have the time,
it took me fucking ages.

Flight Path

Cockatoos and magpie wings
flying bugs and crested things
share the blue, the tufted sky,
perch, respectful, never shy.

Happy to connect with me
content within our sanctuary,
freedom a necessity,
a human/wild fraternity.

Fairy Tales Retold

The Wannabee Duke

There once was a young man called Luke
who fancied himself being a Duke
but exotic mince pies
and all money buys
made the duke in him turn to a puke.

The Pill Taker

In a town in the far away hills
lived a woman who loved taking pills
She had one for a cough and one for a tickle,
one when she ate too much soft bread and pickle
and one for the 'tricity bills!

Fleeced

Mary had a little lamb
who couldn't find his fleece.
He never went to school at all
was never invited to a ball
and finished up marrying his neice!

It's a Lie

Georgy Porgy, truly, no lie
just couldn't stand eatin' a pie!
He loved eating donuts because they were round,
He loved drinking buttermilk with a slurping sound,
He ate lots of biscuits sugary sweet,
But he'd much rather die than eat pie!

Cornered

Little Jacky Horner sat in his corner
eating Miss Muffet's whey.
When she told him to stop and called up a cop
He was frightened and started to say…

I was hungry Miss Muff and you know life is tough,
didn't think you'd miss one bowl of whey.
I am sorry I am, I can make you some jam
with some apples I nicked yesterday!

Night Sky

Oh, little star you've lost your twinkle
wherever did it go?
Did you leave it in a cloud
or in a periwinkle?
Are you trying to get it back,
please look and look and look.
I need your brightly shining light
to read my starry book!

Serves You Right

Ipsy Whipsy loved to climb
he had no fear at all
A challenge would encourage him
to scale a smooth brick wall.
But Ipsy Whipsy couldn't count
he thought his legs were ten,
he tripped one day and broke his head
and spent the whole weekend in bed
while his legs of eight did mend.

Siblings

Jack and Jill were siblings dull
just born to fetch and carry.
They did their work as they were bid,
and not once dared to tarry.

Now one day Jill did mischief seek
when sent up to the well.
'Here, hold the handle, Jack,' she said,
'this pail is heavy as hell.'

And so with pail wide and full
and laughter in their eyes,
the siblings started down the hill
towards a big surprise.

Now Jack whose feet did not have shoes
did fumble and lose his grip
The water sloshed the bucket wobbled,
and Jill began to trip.

Now down they went, a'rolling fast
the empty bucket flew
into the air like a fisherman's cast
as the siblings' fear grew.

'We'll not get supper and it's all your fault!'
said Jill whose fall was broken
by tussocks large and hard as bricks,
her hair all messed and soakin'.

'If you wore shoes upon your feet
instead of stupid rubber,
we'd be at home for sure by now
enjoying evening supper!'

'Oh, shut your face, you stupid moll,
you gave me the heavy side
of the bucket we filled at the well
I'm telling Mum you lied.'

And Jack flew home like a winter wind
left Jill to hold the pail,
'She'll get the blame 'cos she's older than me,'
and Jack prepared his tale.

Eye Blot After Drops

Angels come in many guises
and sometimes bring us big surprises.

Before you draw your own conclusion
or perish the thought, admit confusion,

I must allay doubt and suspicion
by offering up some supposition.

When first I saw this visionary blot,
a side effect of a vodka shot?

No, no, come on! It's morning, mate!
I never drink till evening. Late!

I gazed upon the misty vapour
smudging the humble tissue paper

then closed my eyes and dared to hope.
A sign had crossed my periscope!

An angel wing had touched my eyes.
I'd soon receive my big surprise!

My eyes would see just as before
and open up my visionary door
But woe is me, alas and shit,
the blot was nothing more than spit!

Dusty the Undaunted: an Australian Ballad

(or, the stockman's second coming)

There was movement in the theatre as the surgeon's knife was poised
over where he'd planned to execute his move.
And as he lay unconscious on the narrow table bare
Dusty dreamed of angel wings and horses' hooves.

He was heading home from mustering when the thunderstorm had struck,
the lightning arced across the heavens grey.
Ejected from his saddle like a bullet from a gun,
he landed on his head in yesterday.

Now he wasn't much recalling this adventure on the track,
the pain had gone to ground and he was easy.
But when the Flying Doctor crew had loaded him on board,
he lost his baked bean breakfast hot and greasy.

He didn't see the surgeon shake his head and look defeated,
nor did he hear the sigh of resignation
from the theatre staff assisting in the hope he would survive,
but that was surely just an estimation?

He was Dusty the Undaunted, mustering champion of the ages,
survival was his trusty default setting.
He had no plans to stand before the pearly gates of heaven;
he'd years left for mustering he was betting!

The surgeon, though, knew none of this and prepared to make the call,
the time was three a.m. and all was still,
when suddenly Dusty heaved a sigh that shook the theatre walls,
no bloody way was he going up that Hill!

A miracle had occurred today with the stockman's second coming;
the staff were unprepared and set to flee
Dusty sat with legs aswinging his hair ends all aglow,
'Don't be afraid, my dears, it's only me!'

Wild

Wild as weather in wintry arctic oceans,
wild and hot as father's rage,
wild as rising adolescent emotion,
wild to see the closing of an age.

Wild, insanely as a painful teenage love,
wild as don't care youth,
wild when justice gets the shove,
wild when words don't tell the truth.

Wild when we don't ever get our way,
wild when careless chatter spoils a life,
wild when we are not allowed to say,
wild enough to kill with sharpened knife.

Wild because the earth is changing too,
wild because the climate won't behave,
wild because we don't know what to do,
wild because we see the gathering wave!

Vicious

I'm giving up food,
it's cruel and it's vicious.
I have seen what is done
to make it delicious.

No longer prepared
to watch innocents suffer,
I'll be a Breatharian
a pure and clean puffer.

When we smash avocados
and beat up the cream,
when we chop up the carrots
and strip all the beans,

and crush the poor peanuts,
the proudest of nuts,
and crack the hen's eggs
the cruellest of cuts,

how could we destroy
this beautifully shaped wonder,
by breaking its shell
in an almighty blunder.

And think of tomatoes
boiled then skinned
squashed to a pulp
denatured and thinned.

So I'm giving up food,
I can't stand the pressure
Is it cruel to drink water,
oh, which is the lesser.

These vicious assaults
just have to be stopped,
to protect nature's gifts
being savagely lopped.

They innocently suffer
while we stuff our guts
so it's be kind to vegies
and all nature's nuts!

Wombat Black

Black is the night,
black as the inside
of a wombat's stomach
and nearly as visceral.

Walking through the sticky dark,
a leg slams into a table,
a toe rockets a toy bear
across the landmined room.

Blind as a bat but without radar skills,
I stumble through the power cut,
miraculously finding the bed
somewhere between
the floor and the ceiling.

I slip in between familiar sheets,
lie there corpse still, thinking
there is no difference between
this charcoal night and shuttered eyelids.

Rivers of Tears and Fears

I could

still believe the world is unsullied,
pristine, in mint condition
with a well balanced bright future.

If

Acid rain hadn't fallen,
mining companies had
cleaned up their shit,
rivers hadn't been dammed,
forests had not been destroyed,
animals not been exploited,
oceans not been polluted,
and equal rights had been accorded
to everyone.

I could –

but it wouldn't be true.

Natural Anthem

There's a national song that Australia plays
You can hear it from outback to sea.
You can hear it whenever you walk in the bush
And its spirit is joyful and free.

Sometimes it is strong and sometimes it is wild
Yet it knows to be gentle and giving
To a soul that is worn with the fever of life
To a soul that is tiring of living.

And each time that I walk down a shady bush path
There are whispering notes that surround me
I am cloaked in a symphony so sweet and sublime
With my unbidden dreams far behind me.

Yes, this anthem is sung everyday in the trees,
not just for a special occasion.
It is there when we lift up our heads to the sky,
And provides us with sweet inspiration.

So join with me now in the silence of souls
Let your ears be aware of the story.
Let your body be stroked by the soft passing breeze.
Let your hearts be in love with its glory.

Argelès-sur-Mer

Summer in
Argelès-sur-Mer.
Tourists and locals gather
at the market crêperies,
senses wooed
by the aroma of
lacy, sugary, lemony doilies
of delight.

You and I are there
with hunger of a different kind.
Arms entwined, we breathe in
twilight's moist salty air,
strolling not alone, no but
mingling with other couples
with the same thing
on their minds.

The season of love
catches the unwary
in its net, tangling
hearts and minds,
clouding sensible vision
and holding, before finally
releasing the catch of the day.
into the folds of the marshmallow
duvet, pristine and virginal but
only for a while.

I remember, do you?
Soft utterances of belonging,
whispers of promises,
murmured caresses as skins
touch, shiver with anticipation
beneath the exploring fingers
of new love.

With memories
of old love, I trace
our Mediterranean journey
through the senses and
still see, feel, smell, enjoy
for a few fleeting moments before
the now whisks it all away.

The Spider Saw It All

Little Miss Muffet
one day on her tuffet
was eating some cottage cheese.
There came a horse rider
who started to chide her
and her knickers fell down to her knees.

Now little Miss Muffet
did suffer a buffet
as the rider would soon have his whey.
But she wasn't too scared
even with an arse bared
and asked him how much he would pay.

'I'm giving you nothing
except a good stuffing.
lost all my gold in the war.'
Said she in a huff
being crafty and tough,
'Too bad, but I'm nobody's whore!

Come back later with money
and I'll wait on you, honey,
I've plenty of cheese in my muslin.
If you play your cards right,
serenade me all night.
I might manage some kissin' and nuzzlin'.'

The rider confused,
began to feel used.
He was lonely from years of travelling.
'Cheese makes me feel sick,
so lie down here quick,
my chain mail has started unravelling.'

Now Missy McMuffet
having told him to shove it,
began to feel some sort of pity,
so she lay down beside him
and started to ride him
while singing this quaint little ditty.

Fol de dee, fol de luffet
my name is Miss Muffet,
my forte is making great cheese.
But you, my knight sweet
make a comfortable seat
and my tuffet is eager to please.

Miss Muffet and knight
endured one night,
the moon it was full and romantic.
With the crusader convention
it was not his intention
to prolong any sexual antic.

Two ships in the night
or one night in a ship,
depends on degrees of perspective.
Was Miss Muffett wooed
by this travelling dude
or was he a little defective?

She did give her all
in the hope to enthral
this dashing chain mailed crusader
but his plans had been made
and once she'd been laid
he was off with a cruel 'See you later.'

Not very impressed
satisfied even less,
Miss Muffet put out some fresh feelers.
She wanted a man
with blond hair and a tan
and certainly no wheeler-dealers.

So it came soon to pass
as she sat on her arse,
shelling peas for her family's supper,
that her fortune did lay
in the family way
and not in a crust from the upper.

Now our Missy Muffet
bereft of her tuffet,
she swoons in a pea-shelling dream –
wherein her Prince Charming
is strong and disarming
and definitely right on the beam.

The day it was warm,
bees too tired to swarm
and the noise of pea shelling quite deafening.
Her fingers are numb now,
her conscience says 'Come now,
just get on and stop your cacophoning.'

With eleventy kids,
her life on the skids,
a husband ignoring her needs,
she retreats into dreaming
of a life brightly gleaming
with knights astride stunning white steeds.

Her vision most splendid
on knees slightly bended,
she prays for a happy deliverance
from spuds, peas and kids
that gave her the shits
and were simply a bloody great hindrance.

So Miss Muffet stood fast
finding some strength at last,
she picked up the pot with intent.
With furious aim
and intention to maim,
hubby went down as was meant!

No regrets, no remorse,
she summoned her horse
and swept out the door with her brood.
The wagon was ready
and holding it steady
was son number one Nick the Shrewd.

Now it has to be said
not being well read.
our Miss Muffet's prospects were lean.
No longer a girl
and with grey in her curl,
not too many knights would be keen.

So her son Nick the Shrewd
while in a good mood,
had offered to try find a knight.
But the war had long ended
and differences mended
so nary a knight was in sight.

Nick tethered his horse
to some thick country gorse
and lay down to have a quick nap.
He dreamed of a man
with blond hair and a tan
and more than a comfortable lap.

When he woke with a start
and a fast beating heart,
his dream stood before him a vision!
It was love, he was bitten
and was instantly smitten
but needed to make a decision.

'Dear Mummy,' Nick penned,
'I have a new friend
and I'm sorry I'm not coming home.
No knights to be found,
they are all underground
so you'll just have to make it alone.'

Now her tuffet lies fallow,
her skin has turned sallow,
the memories of bonking are distant.
Yet she still lies there hoping
for some fondling and groping,
her dreams being long and persistent.

But her knight's in a box,
with his chain mail socks,
alone in a grave cold and muddy.
He can't rise to occasion
even with hot persuasion
and Miss Muffet has lost her best buddy.

All her children have fled now,
she has no one to bed now,
the future looks most unattractive.
Still she pines for her lover
so deep under cover,
thus finally rendered inactive.

As Miss Muffet lies ailing,
her best features paling,
she hears a faint knock on the door.
But the ghost does not linger
so she raises a finger
at the white knight she once did adore.

www.ingramcontent.com/pod-product-compliance
Lightning Source LLC
Chambersburg PA
CBHW062205100526
44589CB00014B/1963